Alphabets - Eclectic an
Gallery of Alphabets - Uppercase A

Not Shown - Signal Flags Alphabet

40+ ALPHABETS
including Braille, Hebrew, and Signal Flags

Eclectic

AND

INTERESTING

Charted for Needlework

BY TINK BOORD-DILL

TB-DN

ALPHABETS
For Discerning Makers

20th ANNIVERSARY EDITION
THE GREEN BOOK

Alphabets - Eclectic and Interesting

Acknowledgments

Thank you, Cindy Brown, for introducing me to LoriBeth.

Many heartfelt thanks to Loribeth Etengoff of **Lori's Handmade Magiks,** for helping a fellow designer so graciously and generously.

All rights reserved. No part of this book may be reproduced without written permission from the author.

Stitchers are given permission to enlarge graphs for use as Stitcher's Aids.

©2001 by Tink Board-Dill

©2019 by Tink Board-Dill

(October 17, 2019)

Alphabets - Eclectic and Interesting

Dedication

20th Anniversary Edition

As I readied these books for their new editions, visiting each dedication page has been a wonderful walk down memory lane. Some friends are still with us, while others are not. My mother, my greatest support, is now gone, as are all of my wonderful dogs -- My Big Guys. Still here is Jeffrey, Dear Husband, as we approach our 30th Anniversary. Beppi, our retirement dog, is very different from 'My Big Guys' but every day with him is a treasure and delight... Even while imploring, "Don't be that dog!"

This book is dedicated to all of the wonderful stitchers who bought **Alphabets - Elegant and Unusual**, and clamored for more.

Many thanks to the Shop Owners, for their enthusiasm and encouragement.

Thank you, Miss Deb, for naming this one!

And last but not least, this book is dedicated to my Dear Husband, Jeffrey who is a partner and loving husband, as well as my devoted staff: Tino, Guido and Mams'elle.

ALPHABETS – Eclectic and Interesting
List of Alphabets

Alphabet Name	Suitable for Cross Stitch	Suitable for Tent Stitch	Alphabet Number
Andee26Fancy	✲	✲	Alphabet 1
Andee21Plain and Numbers	✲	✲	Alphabet 2
Arts n Crafts24 Upper Case	✲	✲	Alphabet 3
Arts n Crafts24 Lower Case and Numbers	✲	✲	Alphabet 4
Braille16	✲	✲	Alphabet 5
Braille25	✲	✲	Alphabet 6
Catalog11 Upper Case and Numbers	✲	✲	Alphabet 7
Catalog11 Lower Case	✲	✲	Alphabet 8
DoubleCircleMono19 Upper Case	✲	✲	Alphabet 9
Emmie6 Upper Case and Numbers	✲		Alphabet 10
Flipper18 Lower Case and Numbers	✲	✲	Alphabet 11
Girlie18 Upper Case	✲	✲	Alphabet 12
Girlie18 Lower Case and Numbers	✲	✲	Alphabet 13
Glasgow14 Upper Case and Numbers	✲	✲	Alphabet 14
Hebrew16	✲	✲	Alphabet 15
Instructions25 Upper Case	✲	✲	Alphabet 16
Instructions25 Lower Case and Numbers	✲	✲	Alphabet 17
Jozo24 Upper Case and Numbers	✲	✲	Alphabet 18
Jozo24 Lower Case	✲	✲	Alphabet 19
Loong24 Upper Case	✲	✲	Alphabet 20
Loong24 Lower Case and Numbers	✲	✲	Alphabet 21
Medius18 Upper Case	✲	✲	Alphabet 22
Medius18 Lower Case and Numbers	✲	✲	Alphabet 23
Mere6 Upper Case and Numbers	✲		Alphabet 24

ALPHABETS – Eclectic and Interesting
List of Alphabets

Alphabet Name	Suitable for Cross Stitch	Suitable for Tent Stitch	Alphabet Number
MissM6 Upper Case and Numbers	❦		Alphabet 25
Movies25 Upper Case and Numbers	❦	❦	Alphabet 26
PressedOut18 Upper Case and Numbers	❦	❦	Alphabet 27
Robot20 Upper Case	❦	❦	Alphabet 28
Robot20 Lower Case and Numbers	❦	❦	Alphabet 29
Signal12 Upper Case and Numbers	❦	❦	Alphabet 30
Tempo21 Upper Case	❦	❦	Alphabet 31
Tempo21 Lower Case and Numbers	❦	❦	Alphabet 32
Tinker19 Upper Case	❦	❦	Alphabet 33
Tinker19 Lower Case and Numbers	❦	❦	Alphabet 34
Tinker26 Upper Case	❦	❦	Alphabet 35
Tinker26 Lower Case and Numbers	❦	❦	Alphabet 36
TripleCircleMono17 Upper Case	❦	❦	Alphabet 37
Twirl16 Upper Case	❦	❦	Alphabet 38
Twirl16 Lower Case and Numbers	❦	❦	Alphabet 39
Twirl25 Upper Case	❦	❦	Alphabet 40
Twirl25 Lower Case and Numbers	❦	❦	Alphabet 41
Tyrant24 Upper Case	❦	❦	Alphabet 42
Tyrant24 Lower Case and Numbers	❦	❦	Alphabet 43

Designer's Notes

All of these Alphabets are suitable for Cross Stitch and most are suitable for Tent Stitch.

Some Alphabets can work for Tent Stitch with some additional stitches which have been marked with an **X** symbol.

Any of the Alphabets can be used in Traditional Needlepoint if stitched using a Cross Stitch. When doing this, use fewer plies of thread than in Tent Stitch and make sure that the upper stitch follows the same orientation as the Tent Stitches used.

Andee26 Fancy   Graph 1 of 2

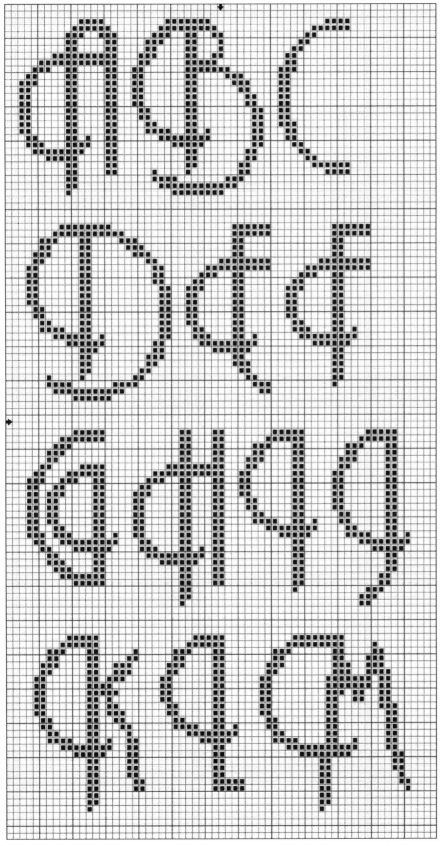

© 2000, 2019 Tink Boord-Dill   Permission is granted to enlarge single copy, solely for use as a Stitcher's Aid.

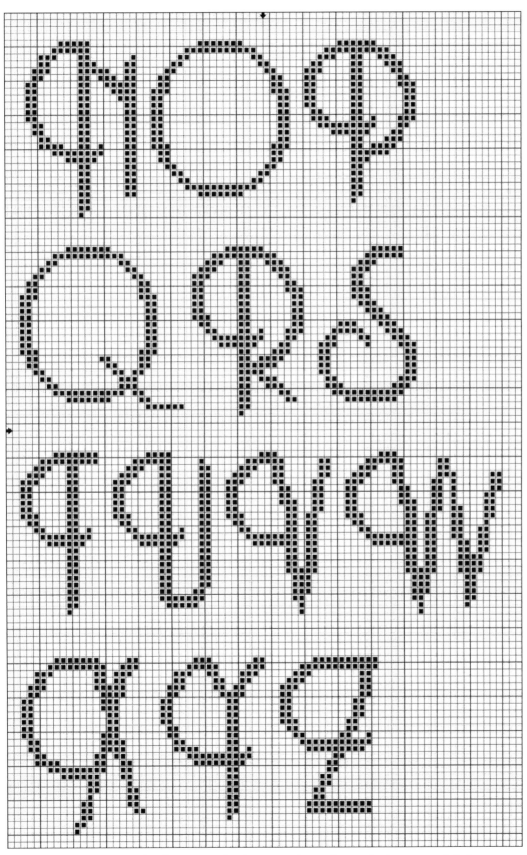

© 2000, 2019 Tink Boord-Dill   Permission is granted to enlarge single copy, solely for use as a Stitcher's Aid.

Andee21 Plain and Numbers   Graph 1 of 2

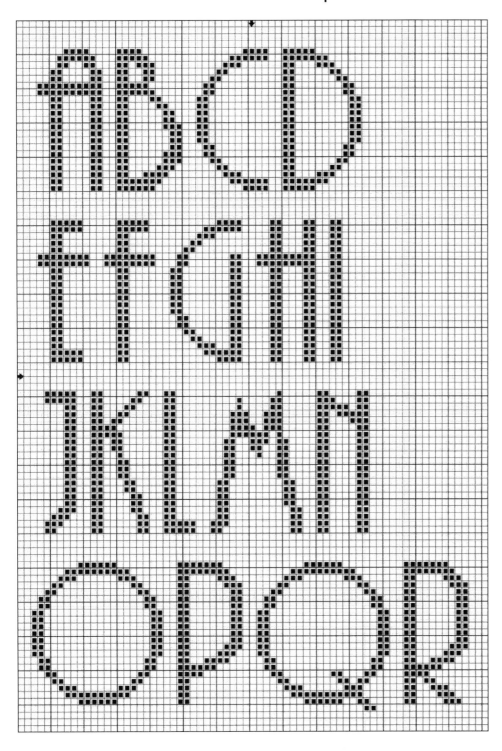

© 2000, 2019 Tink Boord-Dill   Permission is granted to enlarge single copy, solely for use as a Stitcher's Aid.

Andee21 Plain and Numbers   Graph 2 of 2

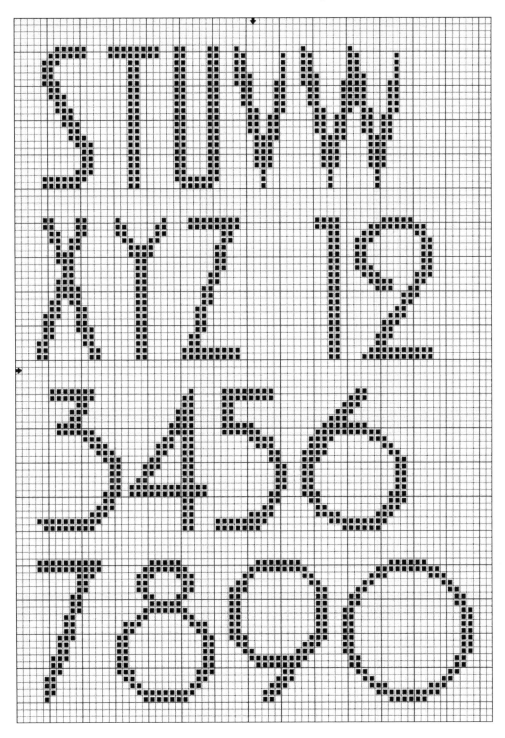

© 2000, 2019 Tink Boord-Dill Permission is granted to enlarge single copy, solely for use as a Stitcher's Aid.

Arts n Crafts24 Upper Case   Graph 1 of 2

© 2000, 2019 Tink Boord-Dill   Permission is granted to enlarge single copy, solely for use as a Stitcher's Aid.

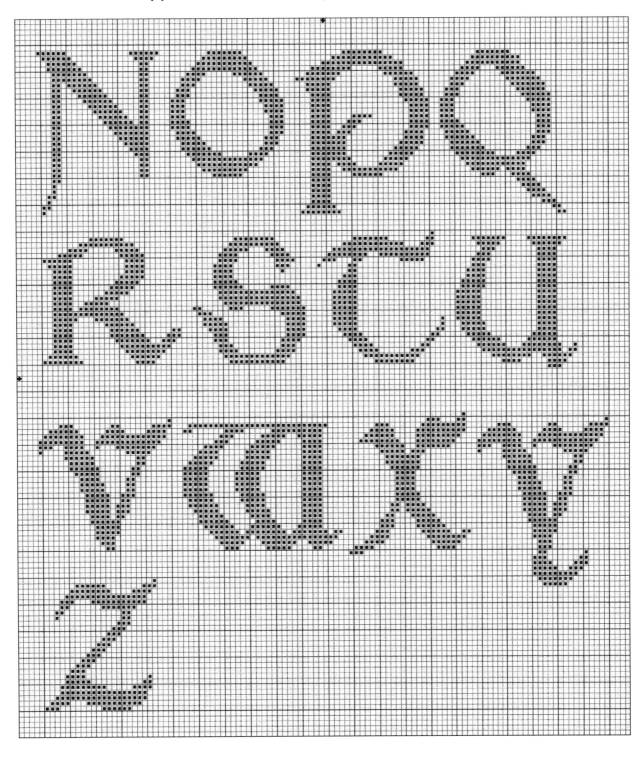

© 2000, 2019 Tink Boord-Dill   Permission is granted to enlarge single copy, solely for use as a Stitcher's Aid.

Arts n Crafts24 Lower Case Graph 1 of 2

© 2000, 2019 Tink Boord-Dill Permission is granted to enlarge single copy, solely for use as a Stitcher's Aid.

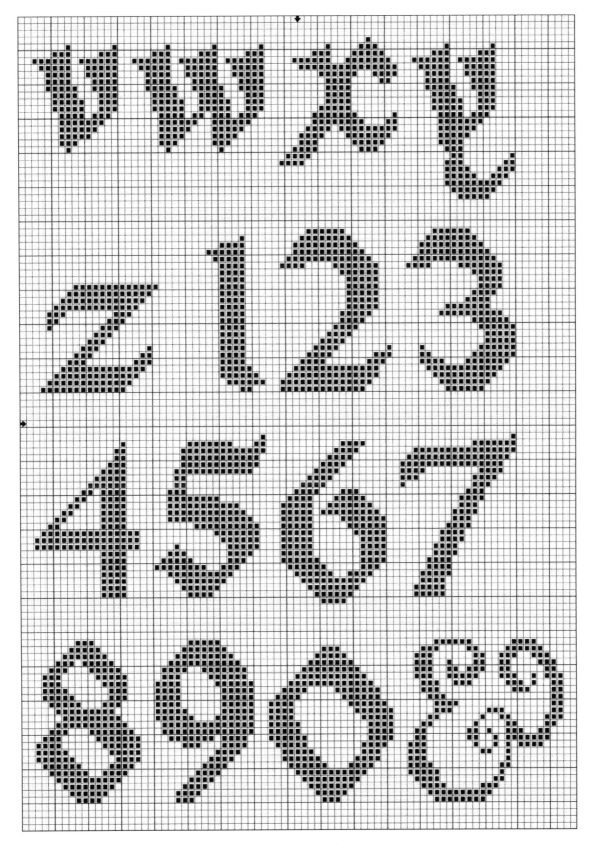

© 2000, 2019 Tink Boord-Dill   Permission is granted to enlarge single copy, solely for use as a Stitcher's Aid.

Braille16   Graph 1 of 2

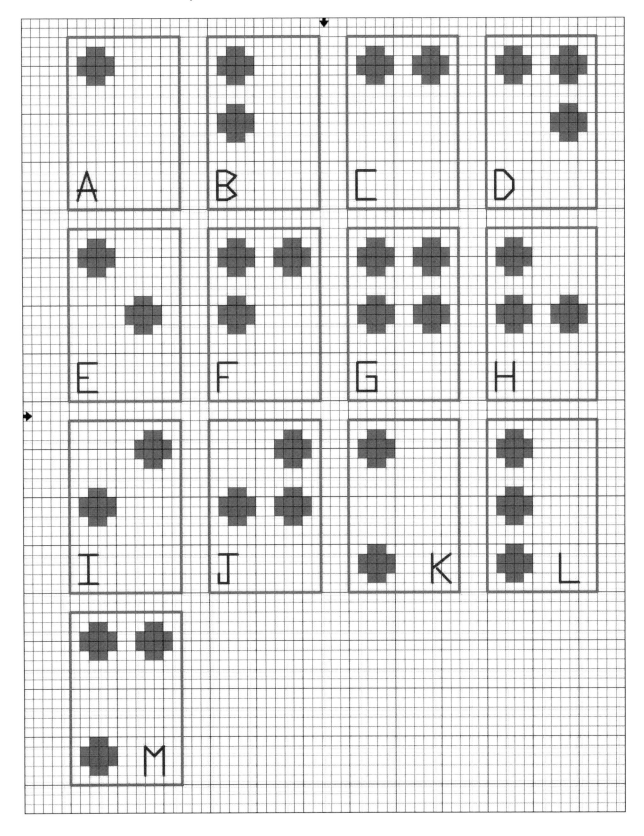

© 2000, 2019 Tink Boord-Dill   Permission is granted to enlarge single copy, solely for use as a Stitcher's Aid.

Braille16　　　　Graph 2 of 2

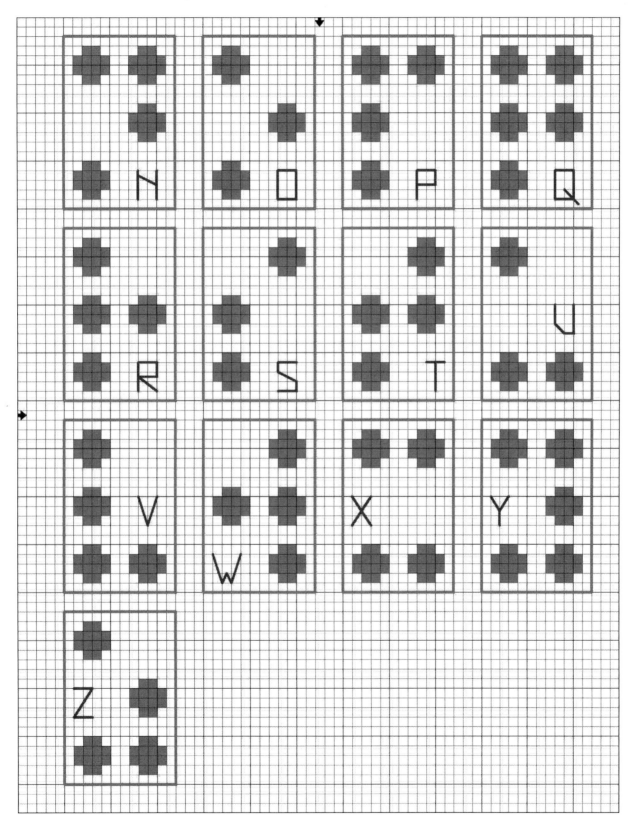

© 2000, 2019 Tink Boord-Dill　Permission is granted to enlarge single copy, solely for use as a Stitcher's Aid.

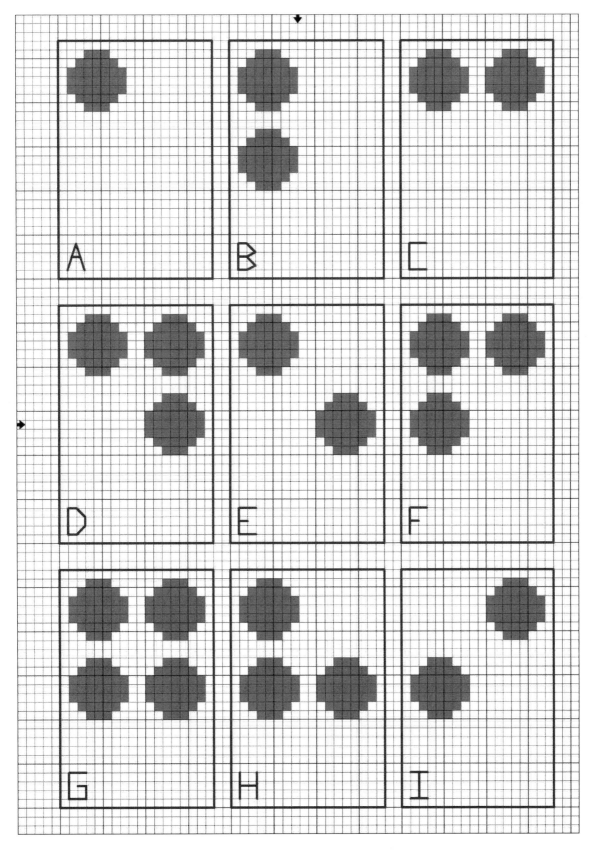

© 2000, 2019 Tink Boord-Dill   Permission is granted to enlarge single copy, solely for use as a Stitcher's Aid.

Braille25   Graph 2 of 3

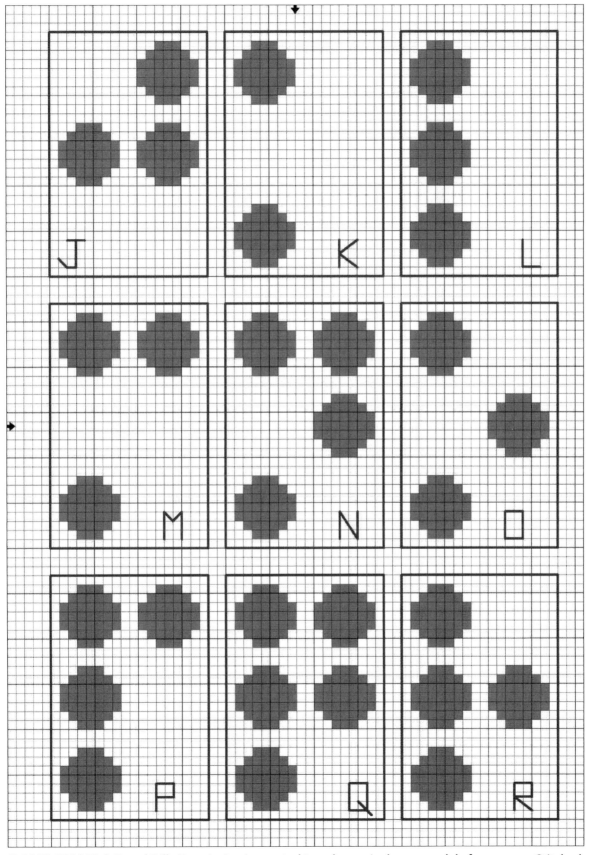

© 2000, 2019 Tink Boord-Dill   Permission is granted to enlarge single copy, solely for use as a Stitcher's Aid.

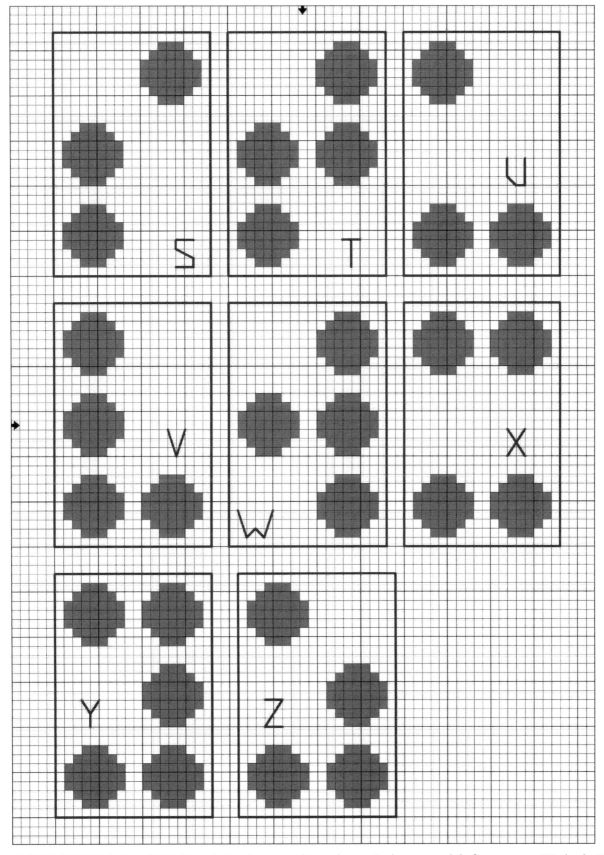

© 2000, 2019 Tink Boord-Dill   Permission is granted to enlarge single copy, solely for use as a Stitcher's Aid.

Catalog11 Upper Case and Numbers

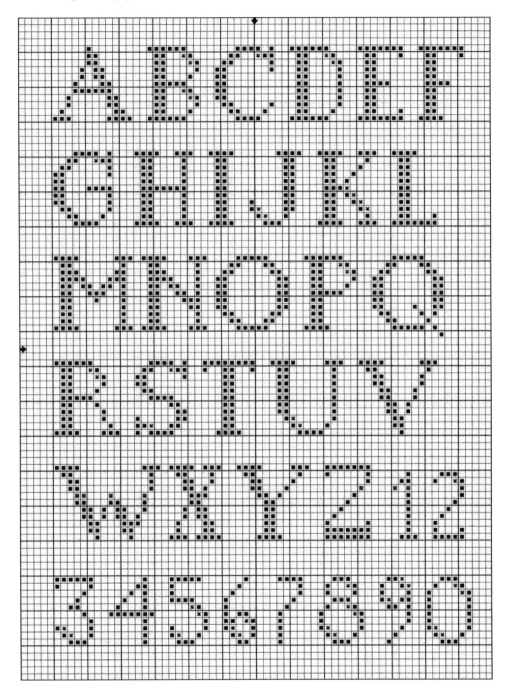

© 2000, 2019 Tink Boord-Dill Permission is granted to enlarge single copy, solely for use as a Stitcher's Aid.

Catalog11 Lower Case

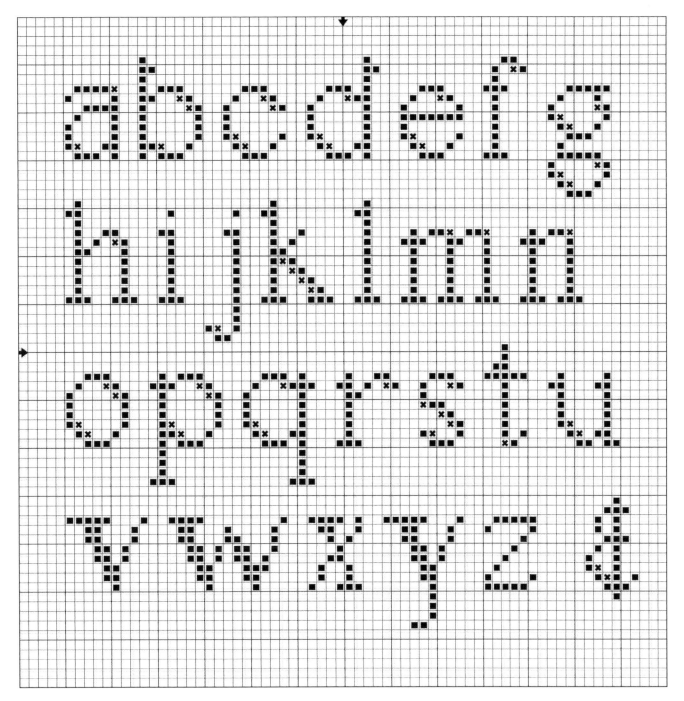

© 2000, 2019 Tink Boord-Dill   Permission is granted to enlarge single copy, solely for use as a Stitcher's Aid.

DoubleCircleMono19 Upper Case   Graph 1 of 2

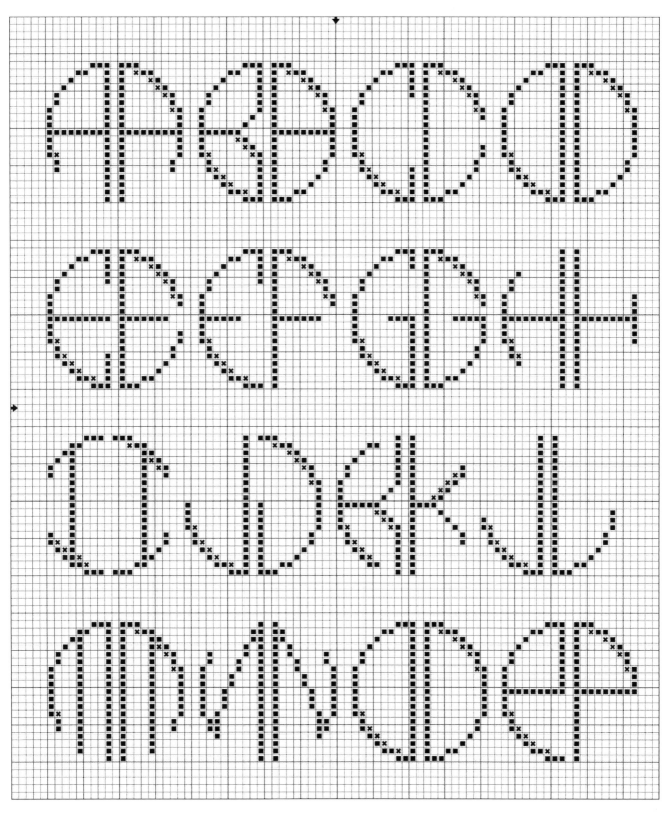

© 2000, 2019 Tink Boord-Dill   Permission is granted to enlarge single copy, solely for use as a Stitcher's Aid.

DoubleCircleMono19 Upper Case   Graph 2 of 2

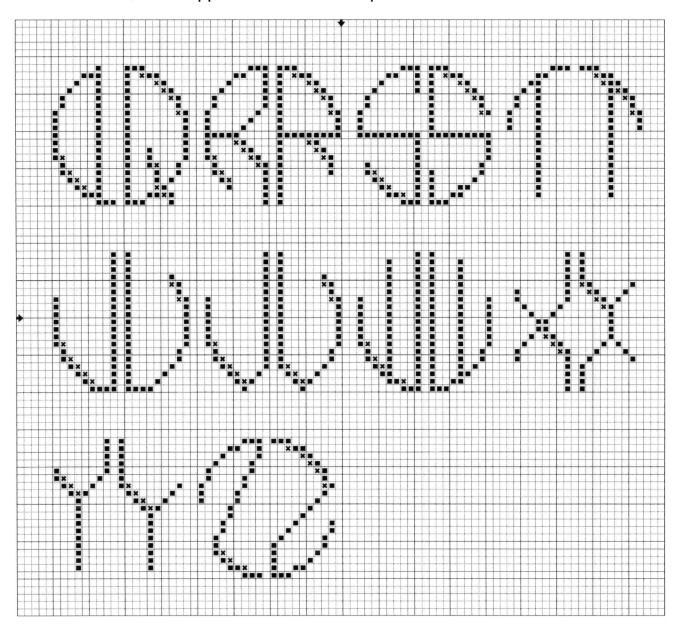

© 2000, 2019 Tink Boord-Dill   Permission is granted to enlarge single copy, solely for use as a Stitcher's Aid.

Emmie6 Upper Case and Numbers

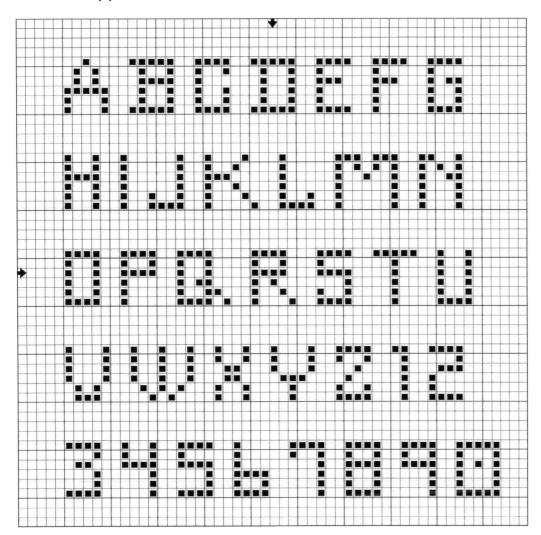

© 2000, 2019 Tink Boord-Dill   Permission is granted to enlarge single copy, solely for use as a Stitcher's Aid.

Flipper18 Lower Case and Numbers   Graph 1 of 2

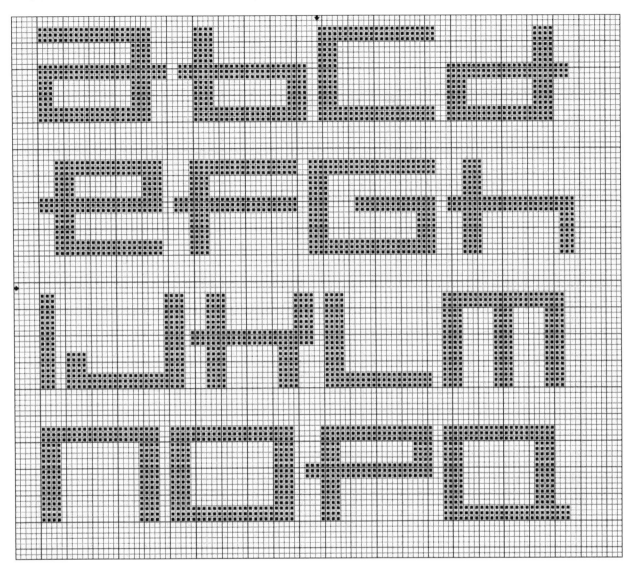

© 2000, 2019 Tink Boord-Dill Permission is granted to enlarge single copy, solely for use as a Stitcher's Aid.

Flipper18 Lower Case and Numbers　　　Graph 2 of 2

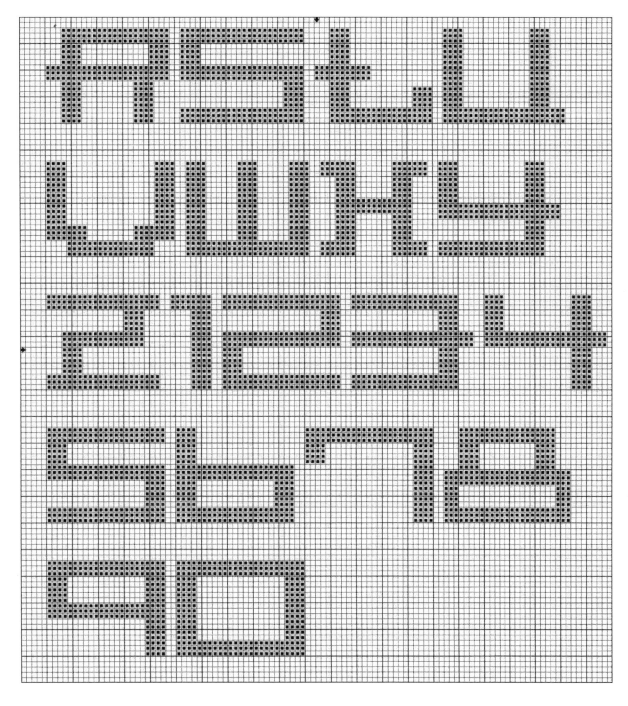

© 2000, 2019 Tink Boord-Dill　Permission is granted to enlarge single copy, solely for use as a Stitcher's Aid.

Girlie18 Upper Case   Graph 1 of 2

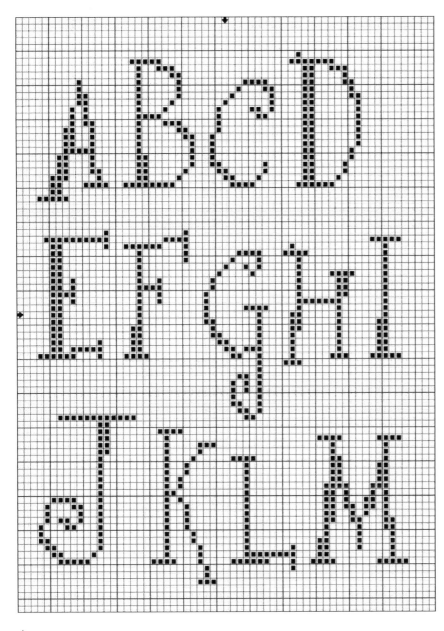

© 2000, 2019 Tink Boord-Dill   Permission is granted to enlarge single copy, solely for use as a Stitcher's Aid.

Girlie18 Upper Case   Graph 2 of 2

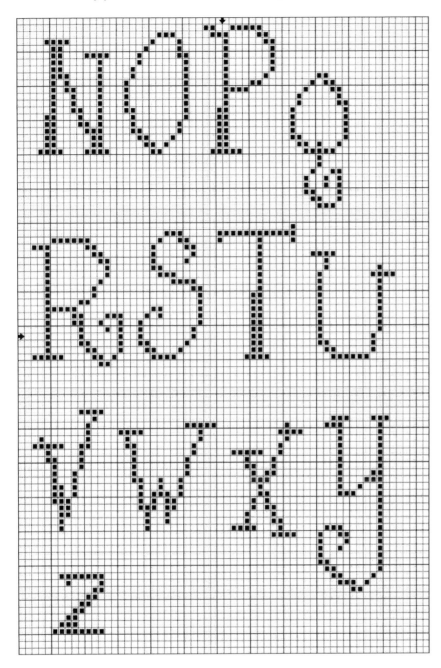

© 2000, 2019 Tink Boord-Dill   Permission is granted to enlarge single copy, solely for use as a Stitcher's Aid.

Girlie18 Lower Case and Numbers   Graph 1 of 2

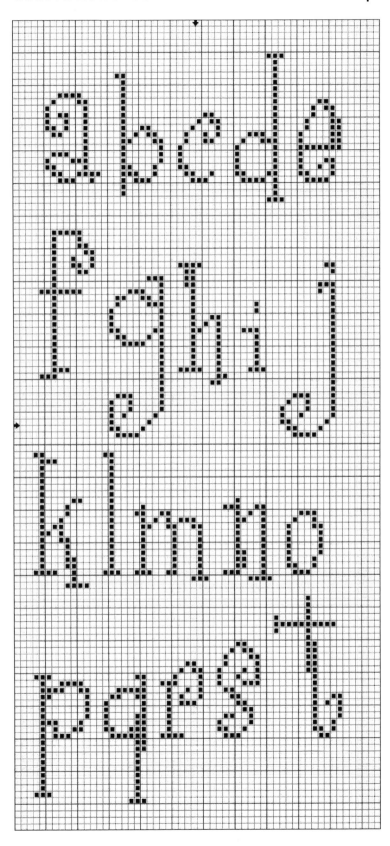

© 2000, 2019 Tink Boord-Dill   Permission is granted to enlarge single copy, solely for use as a Stitcher's Aid.

Girlie18 Lower Case and Numbers   Graph 2 of 2

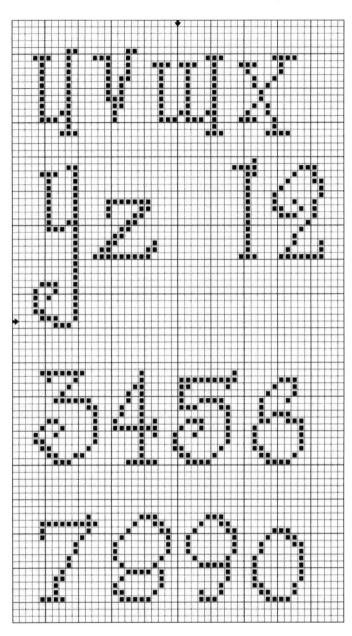

© 2000, 2019 Tink Boord-Dill   Permission is granted to enlarge single copy, solely for use as a Stitcher's Aid.

Glasgow14 Upper Case and Numbers

© 2000, 2019 Tink Boord-Dill   Permission is granted to enlarge single copy, solely for use as a Stitcher's Aid.

Hebrew16 This is a respectful interpretation of the Hebrew Alphabet. Certain symbols may have different forms, depending on their position in a word. I have placed the alternate forms in a box at the end of this chart. Please consult your favorite Hebrew scholar for proper usage.

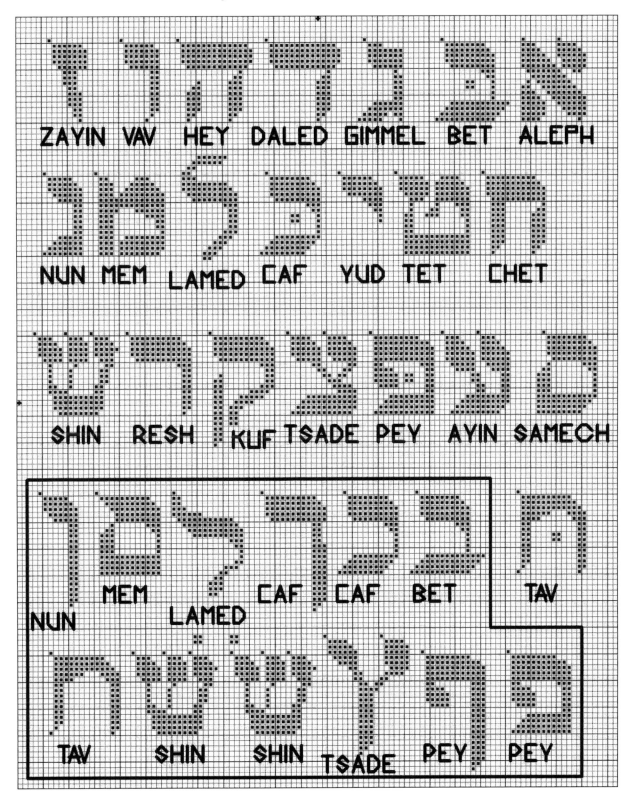

ZAYIN VAV   HEY DALED GIMMEL BET   ALEPH

NUN MEM   LAMED CAF   YUD TET   CHET

SHIN   RESH   KUF TSADE PEY   AYIN SAMECH

NUN   MEM   LAMED   CAF   CAF   BET   TAV

TAV   SHIN   SHIN   TSADE   PEY   PEY

© 2000, 2019 Tink Boord-Dill Permission is granted to enlarge single copy, solely for use as a Stitcher's Aid.

Instructions25 Upper Case   Graph 1 of 2

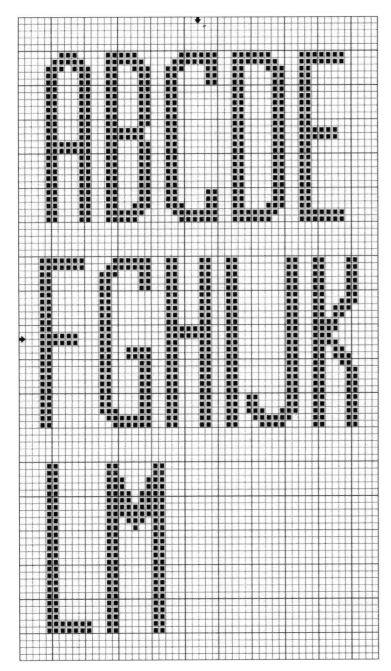

© 2000, 2019 Tink Boord-Dill   Permission is granted to enlarge single copy, solely for use as a Stitcher's Aid.

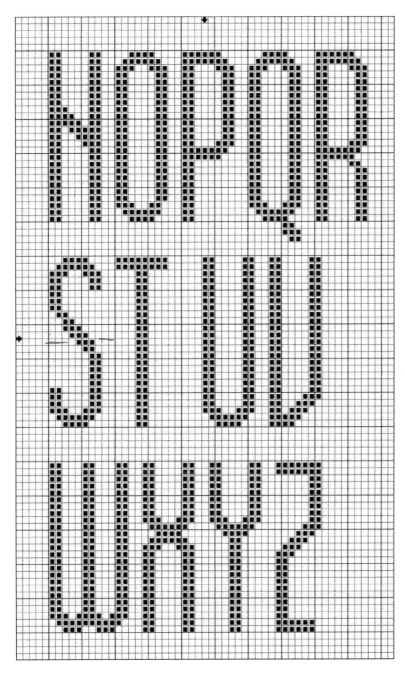

© 2000, 2019 Tink Boord-Dill   Permission is granted to enlarge single copy, solely for use as a Stitcher's Aid.

Instructions25 Lower Case and Numbers   Graph 1 of 2

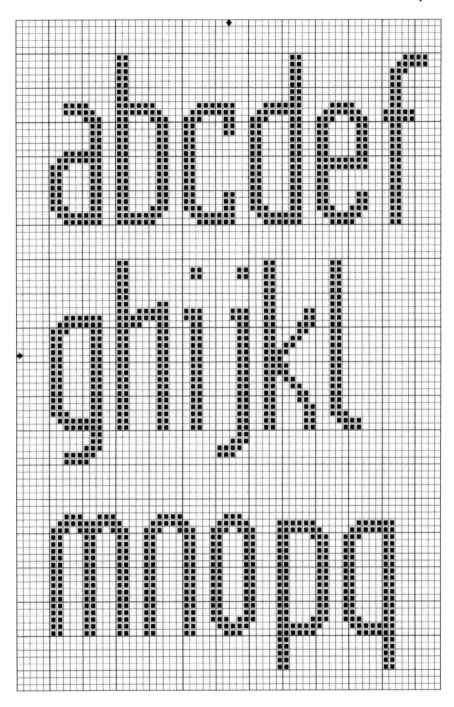

© 2000, 2019 Tink Boord-Dill   Permission is granted to enlarge single copy, solely for use as a Stitcher's Aid.

Instructions25 Lower Case and Numbers   Graph 2 of 2

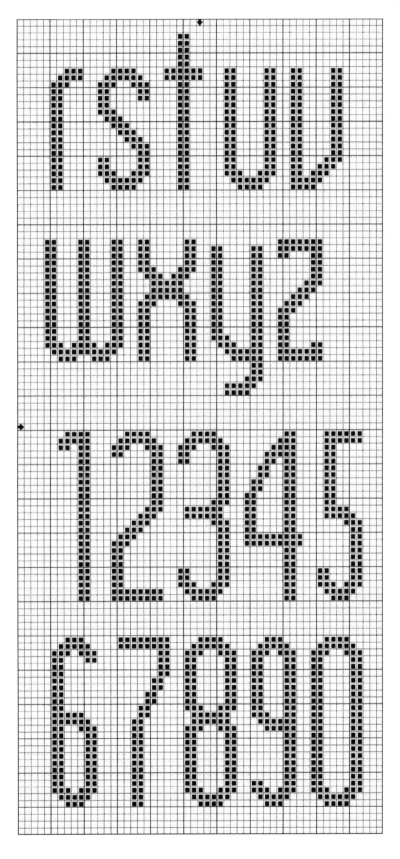

© 2000, 2019 Tink Boord-Dill   Permission is granted to enlarge single copy, solely for use as a Stitcher's Aid.

Jozo24 Upper Case   Graph 1 of 2

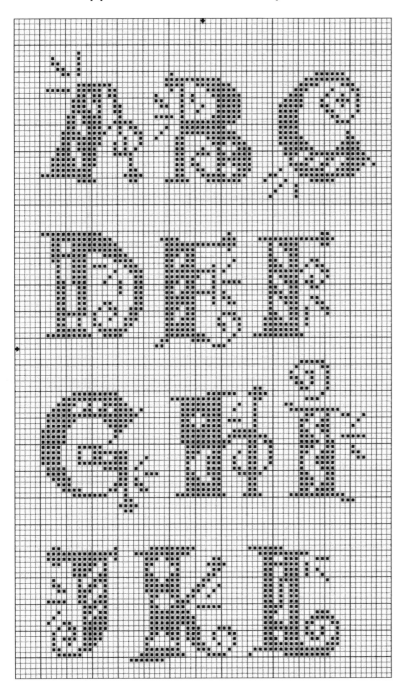

© 2000, 2019 Tink Boord-Dill   Permission is granted to enlarge single copy, solely for use as a Stitcher's Aid.

Jozo24 Upper Case   Graph 2 of 2

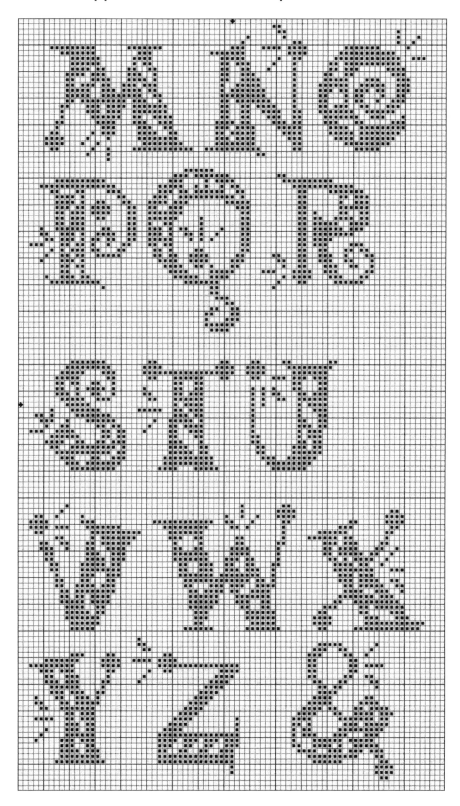

© 2000, 2019 Tink Boord-Dill   Permission is granted to enlarge single copy, solely for use as a Stitcher's Aid.

Jozo24 Lower Case and Numbers   Graph 1 of 2

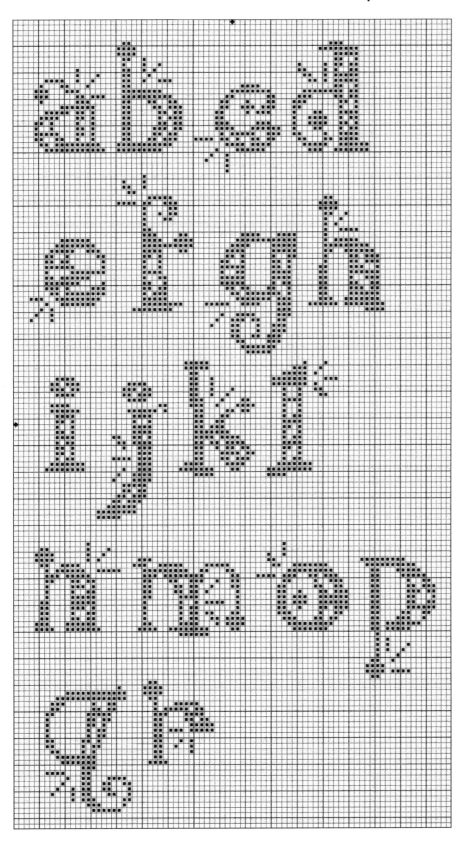

© 2000, 2019 Tink Boord-Dill   Permission is granted to enlarge single copy, solely for use as a Stitcher's Aid.

Jozo24 Lower Case and Numbers   Graph 2 of 2

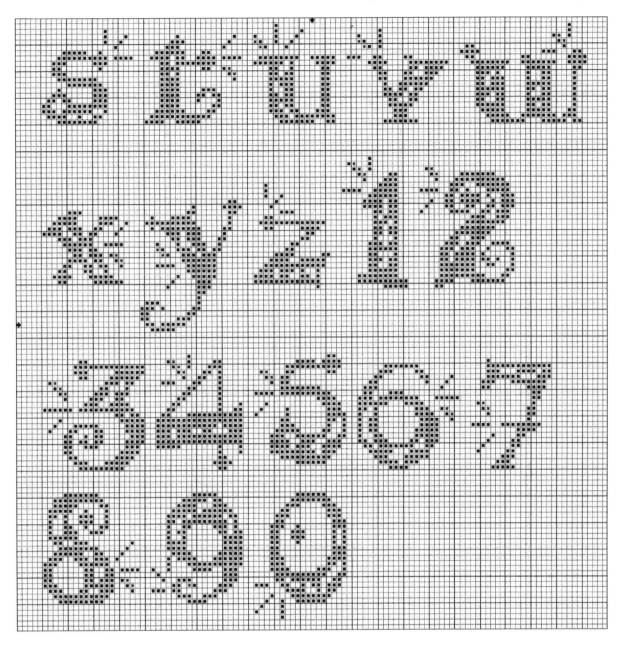

© 2000, 2019 Tink Boord-Dill   Permission is granted to enlarge single copy, solely for use as a Stitcher's Aid.

Loong24 Upper Case   Graph 1 of 2

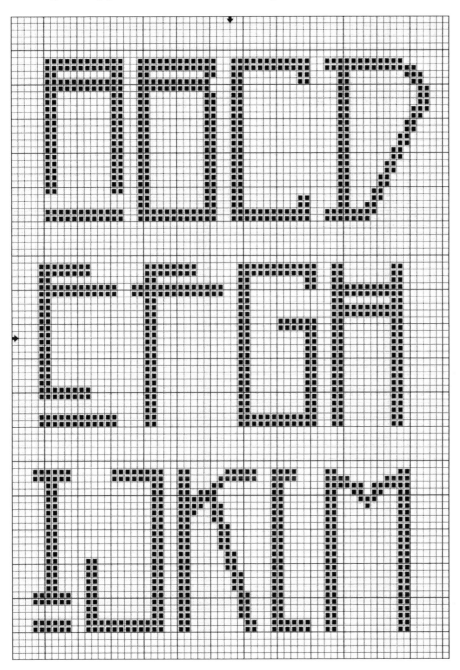

© 2000, 2019 Tink Boord-Dill   Permission is granted to enlarge single copy, solely for use as a Stitcher's Aid.

Loong24 Upper Case   Graph 2 of 2

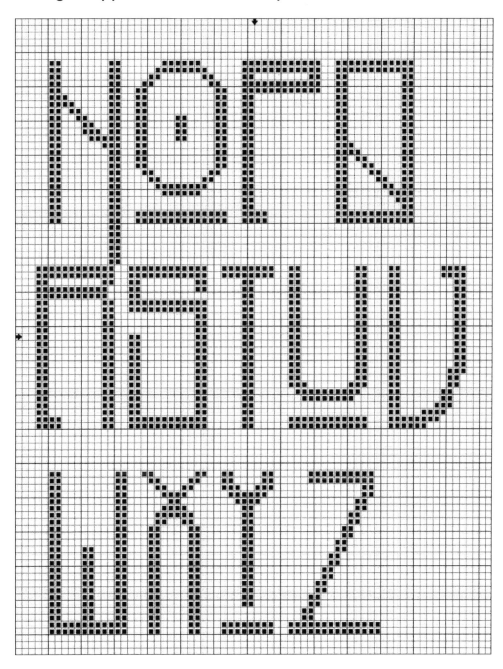

© 2000, 2019 Tink Boord-Dill   Permission is granted to enlarge single copy, solely for use as a Stitcher's Aid.

Loong24 Lower Case and Numbers   Graph 1 of 2

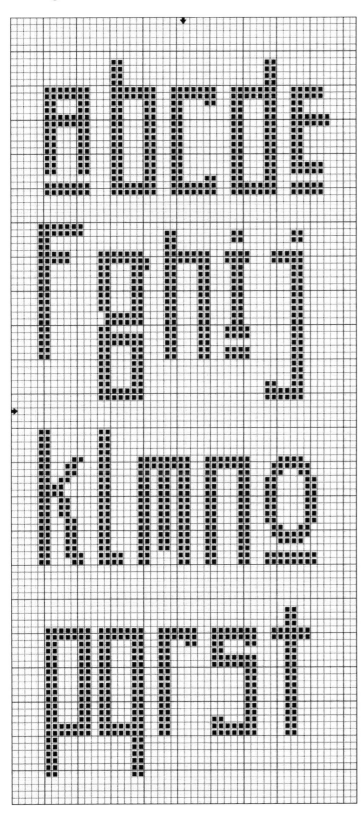

© 2000, 2019 Tink Boord-Dill   Permission is granted to enlarge single copy, solely for use as a Stitcher's Aid.

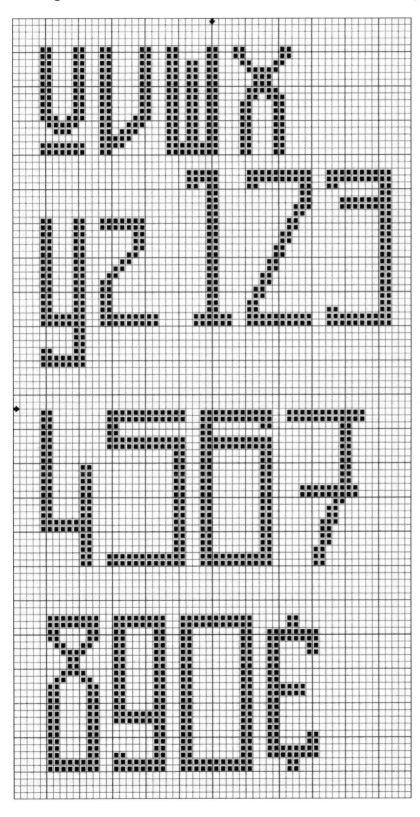

© 2000, 2019 Tink Boord-Dill   Permission is granted to enlarge single copy, solely for use as a Stitcher's Aid.

Medius18 Upper Case   Graph 1 of 2

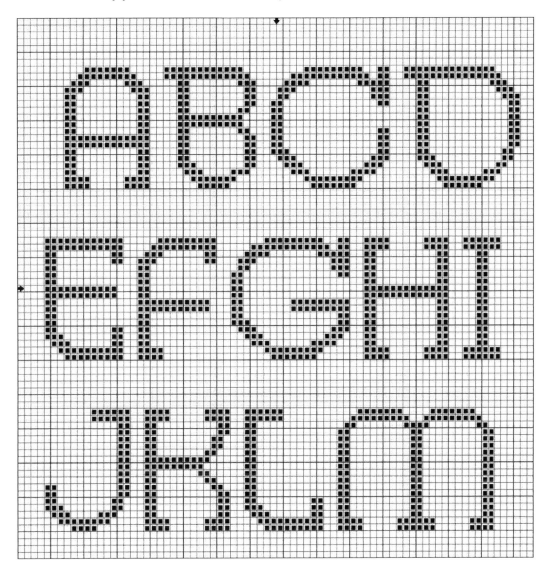

© 2000, 2019 Tink Boord-Dill   Permission is granted to enlarge single copy, solely for use as a Stitcher's Aid.

Medius18 Upper Case   Graph 2 of 2

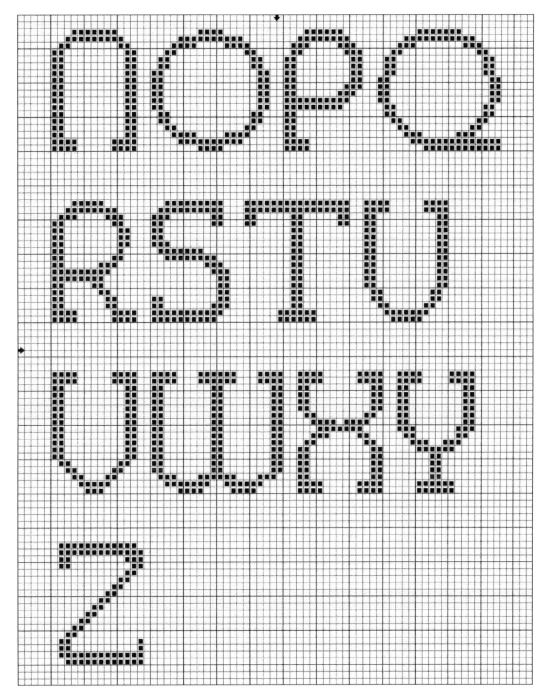

© 2000, 2019 Tink Boord-Dill   Permission is granted to enlarge single copy, solely for use as a Stitcher's Aid.

Medius18 Lower Case and Numbers   Graph 1 of 2

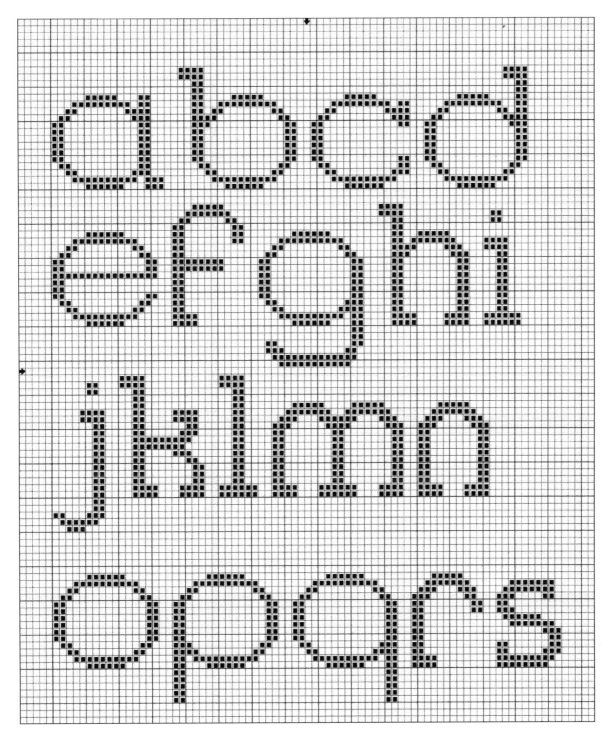

© 2000, 2019 Tink Boord-Dill   Permission is granted to enlarge single copy, solely for use as a Stitcher's Aid.

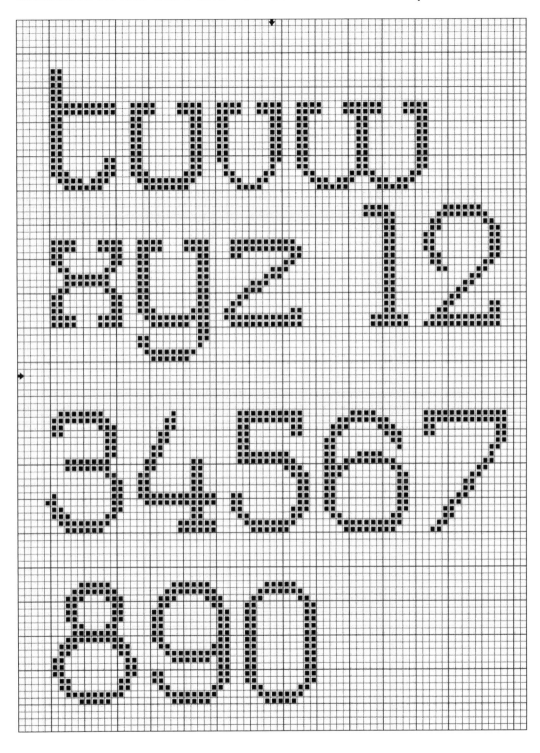

© 2000, 2019 Tink Boord-Dill   Permission is granted to enlarge single copy, solely for use as a Stitcher's Aid.

Mere6 Upper Case and Numbers

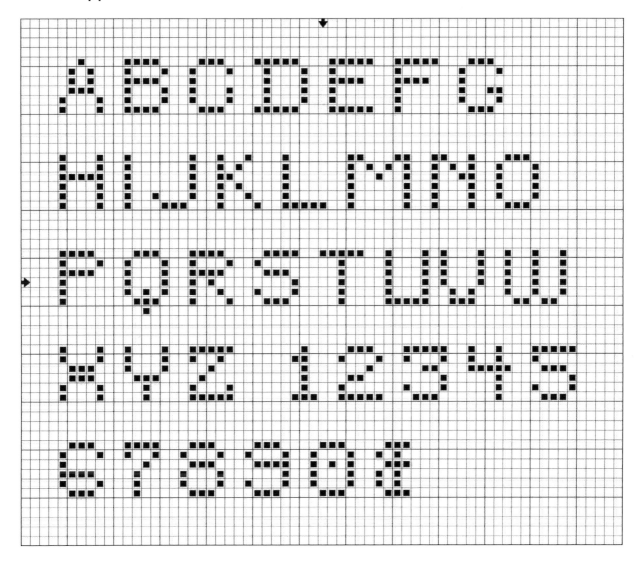

© 2000, 2019 Tink Boord-Dill   Permission is granted to enlarge single copy, solely for use as a Stitcher's Aid.

MissM6 Upper Case and Numbers

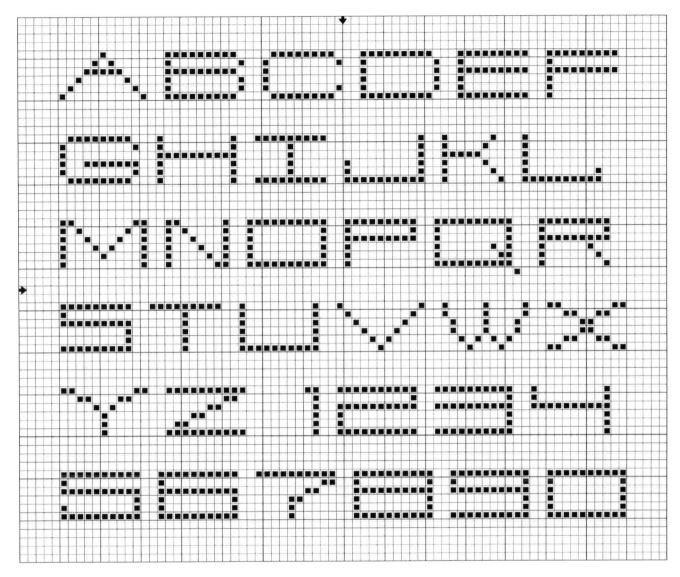

© 2000, 2019 Tink Boord-Dill   Permission is granted to enlarge single copy, solely for use as a Stitcher's Aid.

Movies25 Upper Case and Numbers   Graph 1 of 2

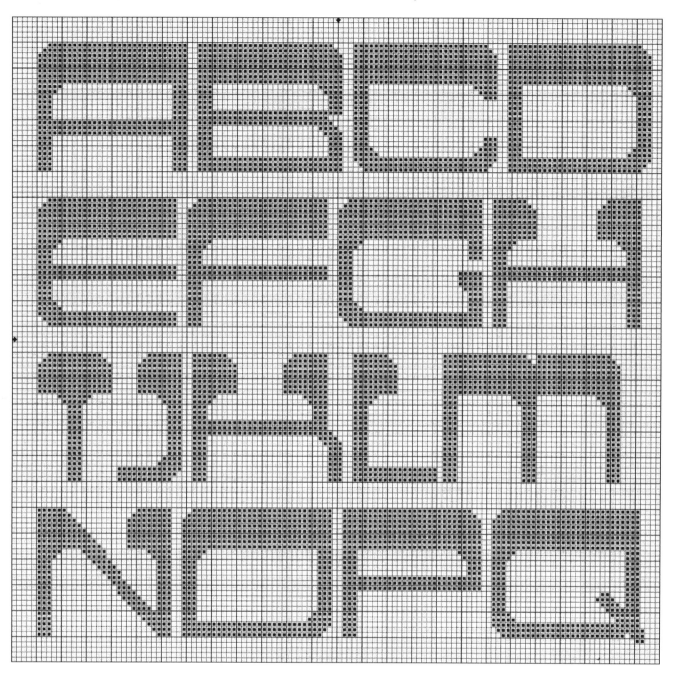

© 2000, 2019 Tink Boord-Dill   Permission is granted to enlarge single copy, solely for use as a Stitcher's Aid.

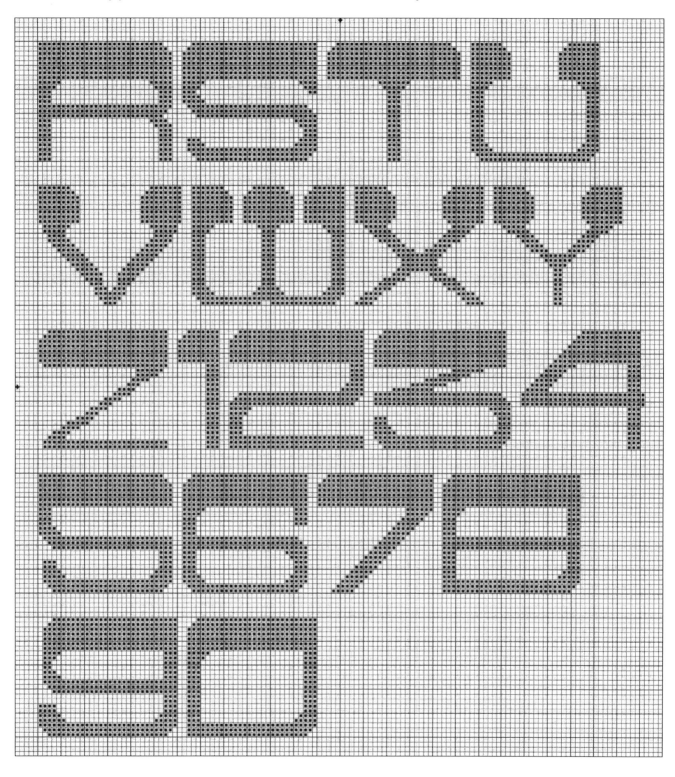

© 2000, 2019 Tink Boord-Dill   Permission is granted to enlarge single copy, solely for use as a Stitcher's Aid.

PressedOut18 Upper Case and Numbers   Graph 1 of 2

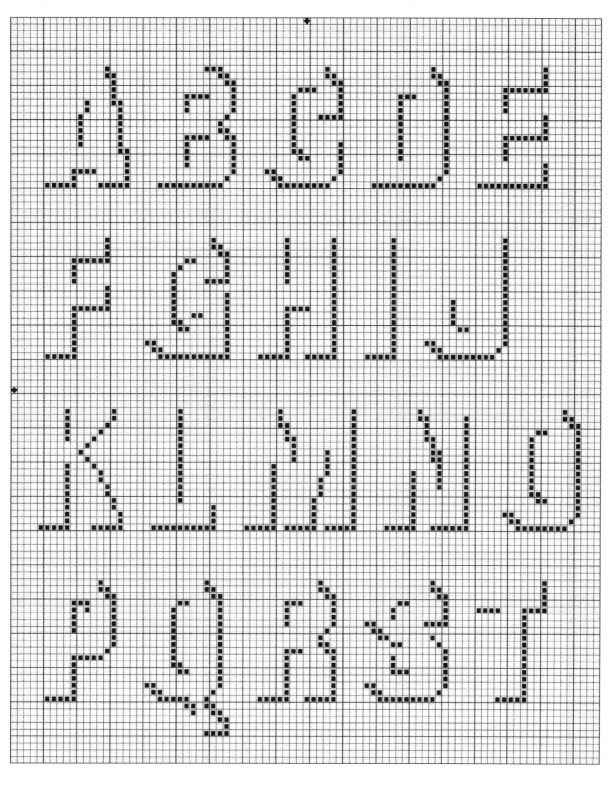

© 2000, 2019 Tink Boord-Dill   Permission is granted to enlarge single copy, solely for use as a Stitcher's Aid.

PressedOut18 Upper Case and Numbers   Graph 2 of 2

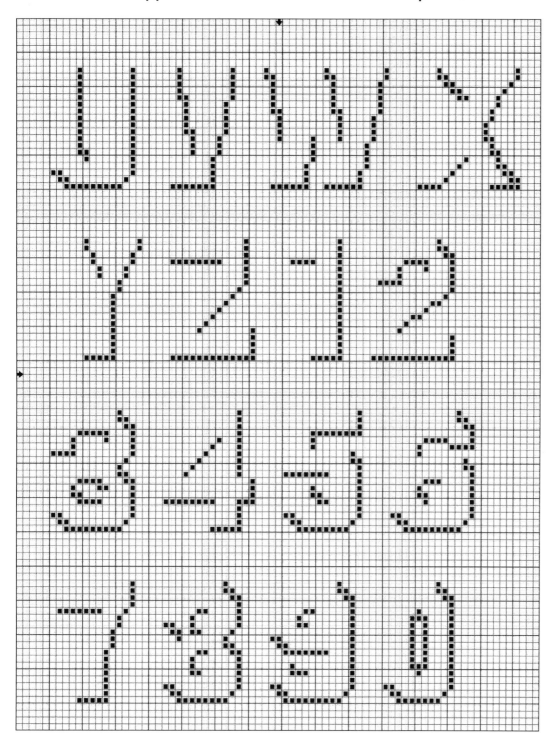

© 2000, 2019 Tink Boord-Dill   Permission is granted to enlarge single copy, solely for use as a Stitcher's Aid.

Robot20 Upper Case   Graph 1 of 2

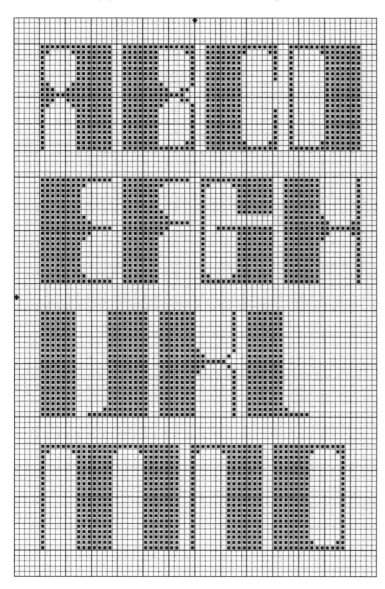

© 2000, 2019 Tink Boord-Dill   Permission is granted to enlarge single copy, solely for use as a Stitcher's Aid.

Robot20 Upper Case   Graph 2 of 2

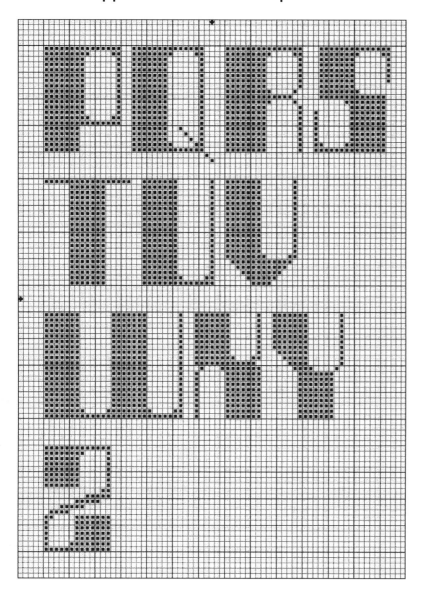

© 2000, 2019 Tink Boord-Dill   Permission is granted to enlarge single copy, solely for use as a Stitcher's Aid.

Robot20 Lower Case and Numbers   Graph 1 of 2

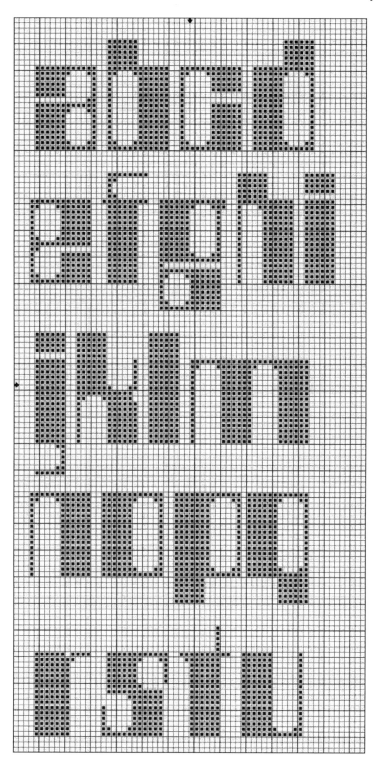

© 2000, 2019 Tink Boord-Dill   Permission is granted to enlarge single copy, solely for use as a Stitcher's Aid.

Robot20 Lower Case and Numbers   Graph 2 of 2

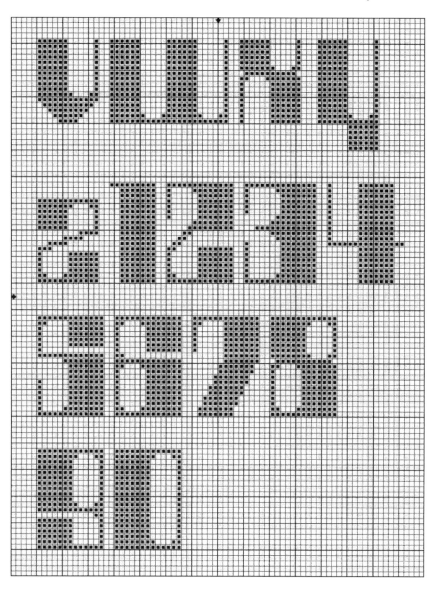

© 2000, 2019 Tink Boord-Dill   Permission is granted to enlarge single copy, solely for use as a Stitcher's Aid.

Signal12 Upper Case and Numbers   Graph 1 of 2

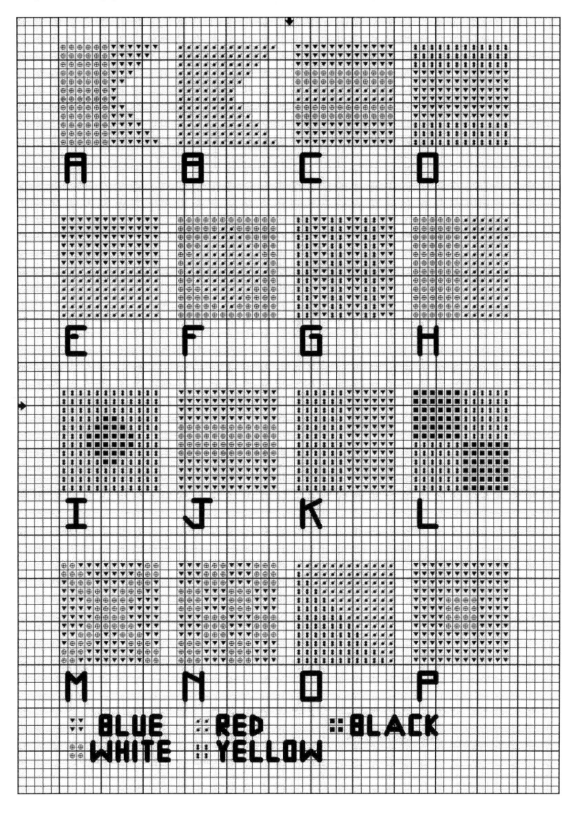

© 2000, 2019 Tink Boord-Dill   Permission is granted to enlarge single copy, solely for use as a Stitcher's Aid.

Signal12 Upper Case and Numbers   Graph 2 of 2

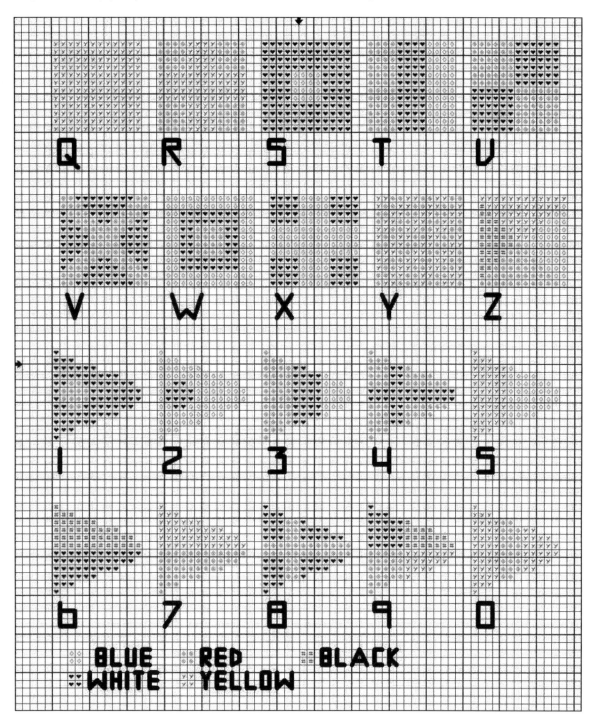

© 2000, 2019 Tink Boord-Dill   Permission is granted to enlarge single copy, solely for use as a Stitcher's Aid.

Tempo21 Upper Case

© 2000, 2019 Tink Boord-Dill   Permission is granted to enlarge single copy, solely for use as a Stitcher's Aid.

Tempo21 Lower Case and Numbers   Graph 1 of 2

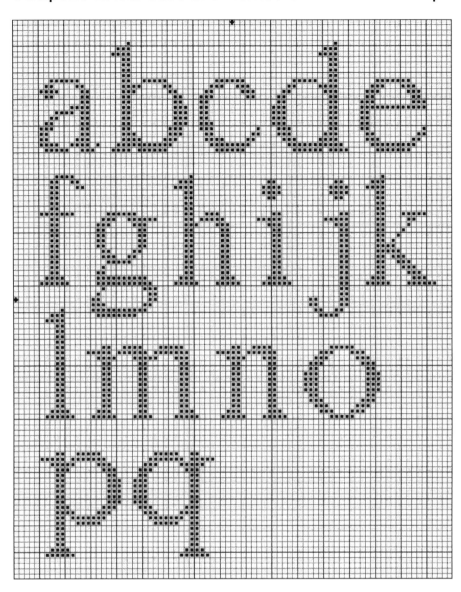

© 2000, 2019 Tink Boord-Dill   Permission is granted to enlarge single copy, solely for use as a Stitcher's Aid.

Tempo21 Lower Case and Numbers   Graph 2 of 2

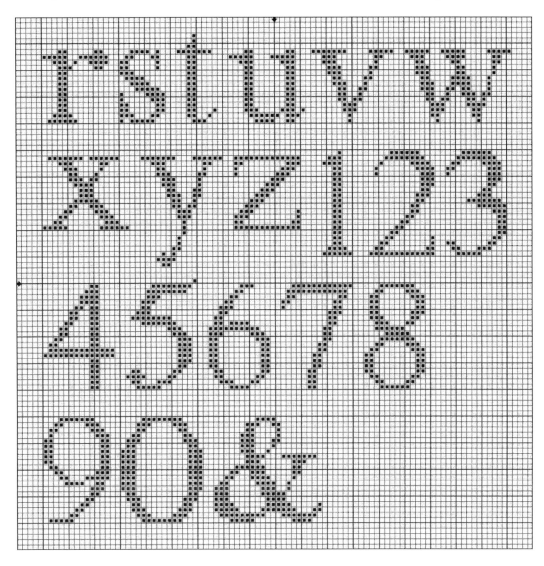

© 2000, 2019 Tink Boord-Dill   Permission is granted to enlarge single copy, solely for use as a Stitcher's Aid.

Tinker19 Upper Case   Graph 1 of 2

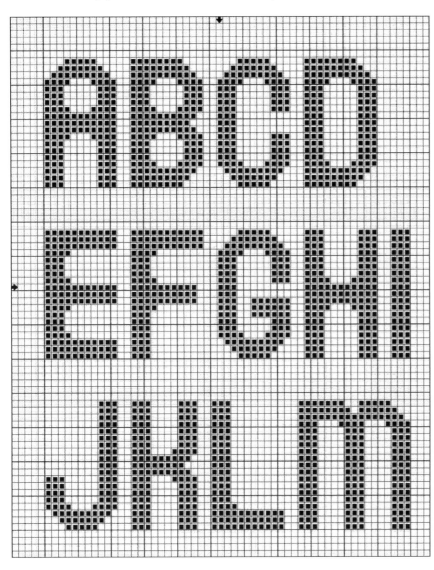

© 2000, 2019 Tink Boord-Dill   Permission is granted to enlarge single copy, solely for use as a Stitcher's Aid.

Tinker19 Upper Case   Graph 2 of 2

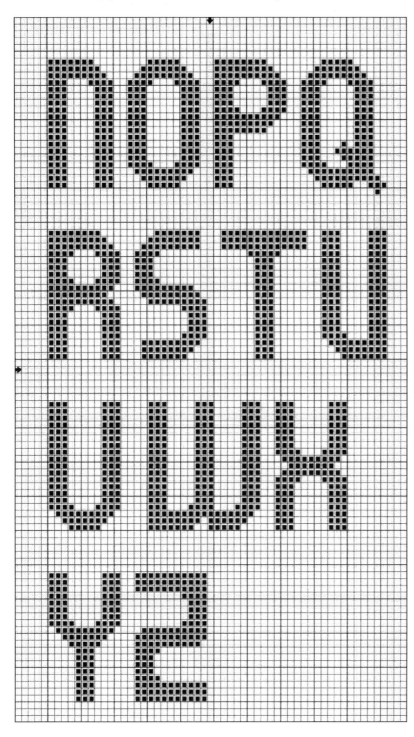

© 2000, 2019 Tink Boord-Dill   Permission is granted to enlarge single copy, solely for use as a Stitcher's Aid.

Tinker19 Lower Case and Numbers   Graph 1 of 2

© 2000, 2019 Tink Boord-Dill   Permission is granted to enlarge single copy, solely for use as a Stitcher's Aid.

Tinker19 Lower Case and Numbers   Graph 2 of 2

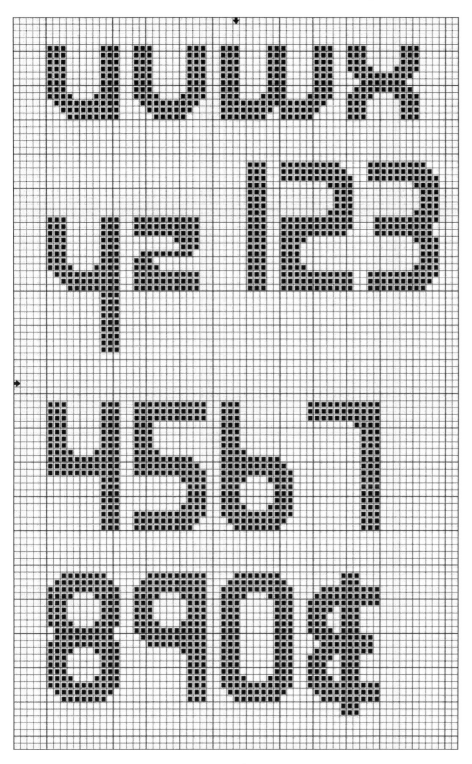

© 2000, 2019 Tink Boord-Dill   Permission is granted to enlarge single copy, solely for use as a Stitcher's Aid.

Tinker26 Upper Case   Graph 1 of 2

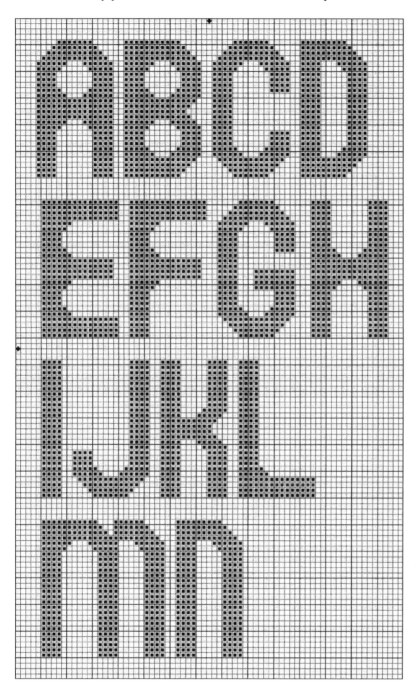

© 2000, 2019 Tink Boord-Dill   Permission is granted to enlarge single copy, solely for use as a Stitcher's Aid.

Tinker26 Upper Case　　　　　　　Graph 2 of 2

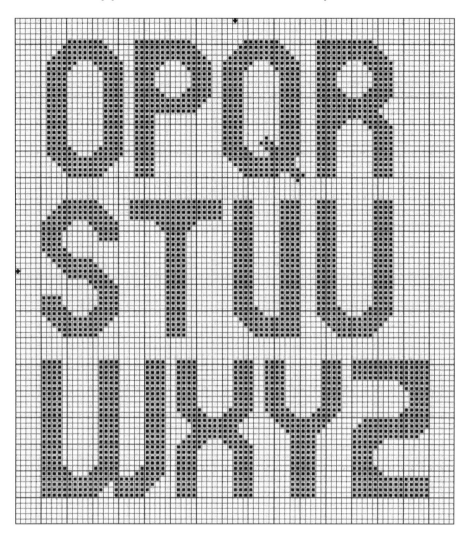

© 2000, 2019 Tink Boord-Dill　Permission is granted to enlarge single copy, solely for use as a Stitcher's Aid.

Tinker26 Lower Case and Numbers   Graph 1 of 2

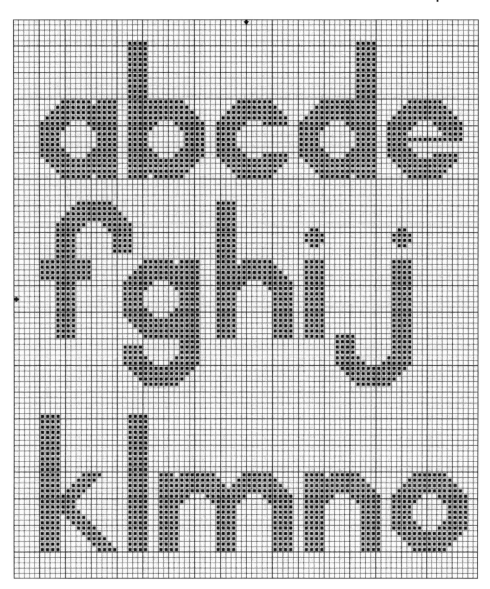

© 2000, 2019 Tink Boord-Dill   Permission is granted to enlarge single copy, solely for use as a Stitcher's Aid.

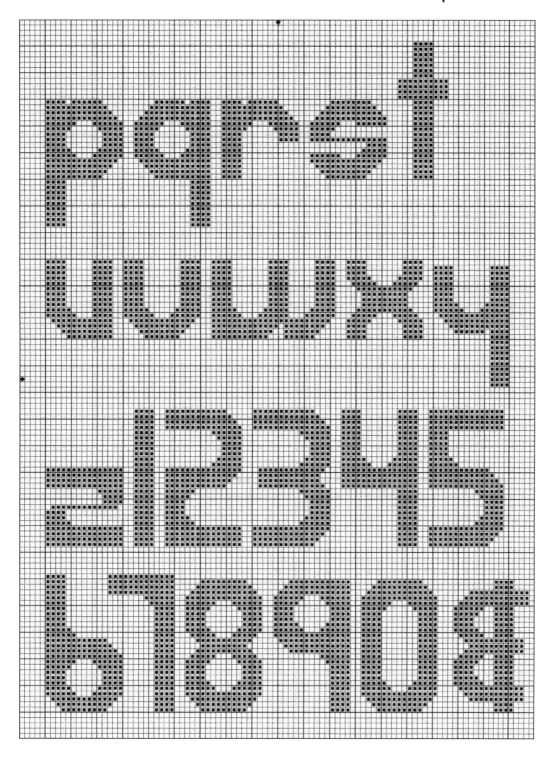

© 2000, 2019 Tink Boord-Dill   Permission is granted to enlarge single copy, solely for use as a Stitcher's Aid.

TripleCircleMono17 Upper Case   Graph 1 of 2

© 2000, 2019 Tink Boord-Dill   Permission is granted to enlarge single copy, solely for use as a Stitcher's Aid.

TripleCircleMono17 Upper Case　　　　Graph 2 of 2

© 2000, 2019 Tink Boord-Dill　Permission is granted to enlarge single copy, solely for use as a Stitcher's Aid.

Twirl16 Upper Case

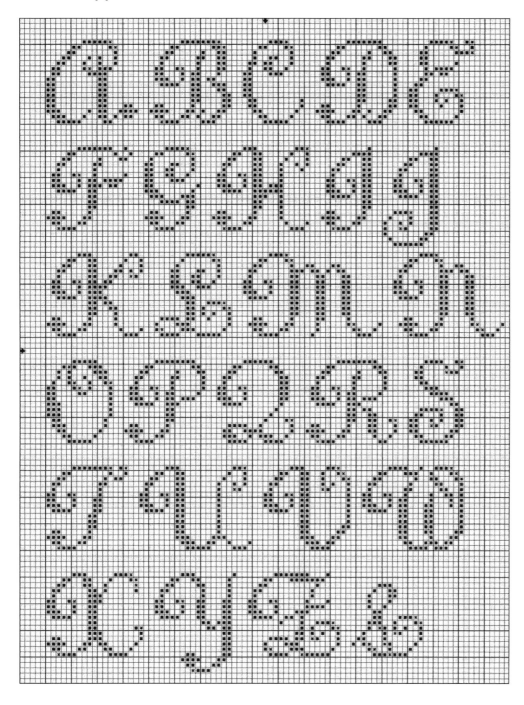

© 2000, 2019 Tink Boord-Dill   Permission is granted to enlarge single copy, solely for use as a Stitcher's Aid.

Twirl16 Lower Case and Numbers

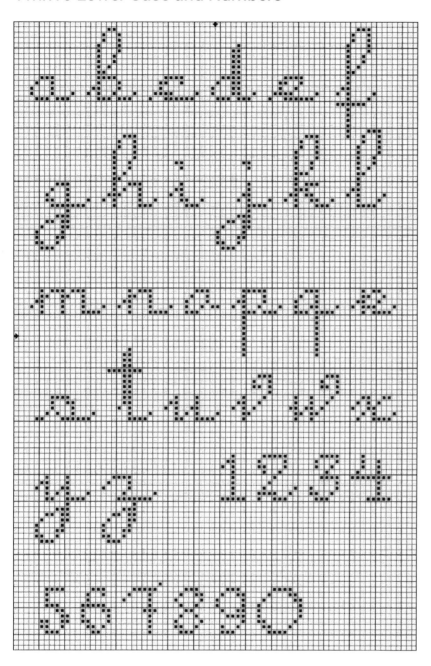

© 2000, 2019 Tink Boord-Dill   Permission is granted to enlarge single copy, solely for use as a Stitcher's Aid.

Twirl25 Upper Case   Graph 1 of 2

© 2000, 2019 Tink Boord-Dill   Permission is granted to enlarge single copy, solely for use as a Stitcher's Aid.

© 2000, 2019 Tink Boord-Dill   Permission is granted to enlarge single copy, solely for use as a Stitcher's Aid.

Twirl25 Lower Case and Numbers

© 2000, 2019 Tink Boord-Dill　Permission is granted to enlarge single copy, solely for use as a Stitcher's Aid.

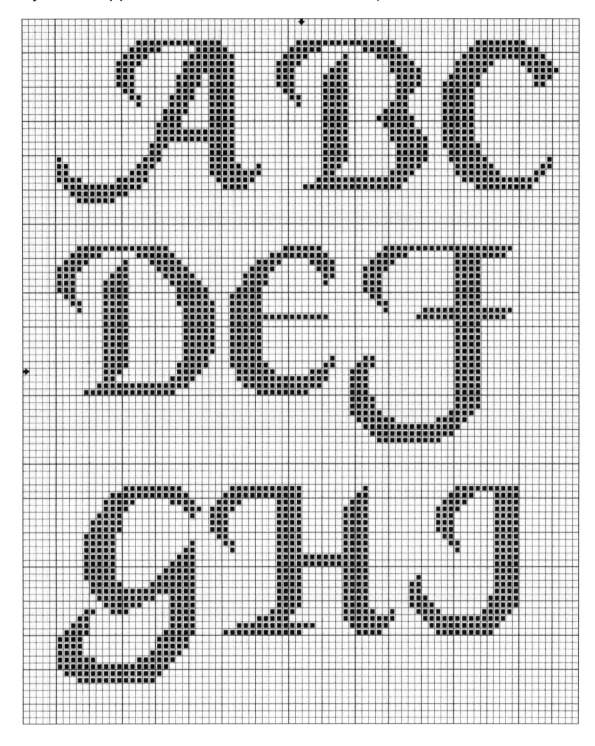

© 2000, 2019 Tink Boord-Dill   Permission is granted to enlarge single copy, solely for use as a Stitcher's Aid.

© 2000, 2019 Tink Boord-Dill   Permission is granted to enlarge single copy, solely for use as a Stitcher's Aid.

Tyrant24 Upper Case   Graph 3 of 3

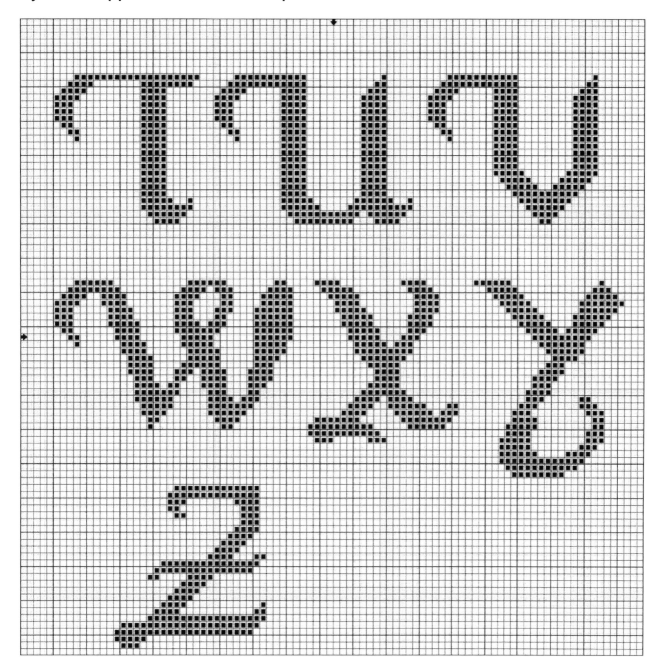

© 2000, 2019 Tink Boord-Dill   Permission is granted to enlarge single copy, solely for use as a Stitcher's Aid.

© 2000, 2019 Tink Boord-Dill   Permission is granted to enlarge single copy, solely for use as a Stitcher's Aid.

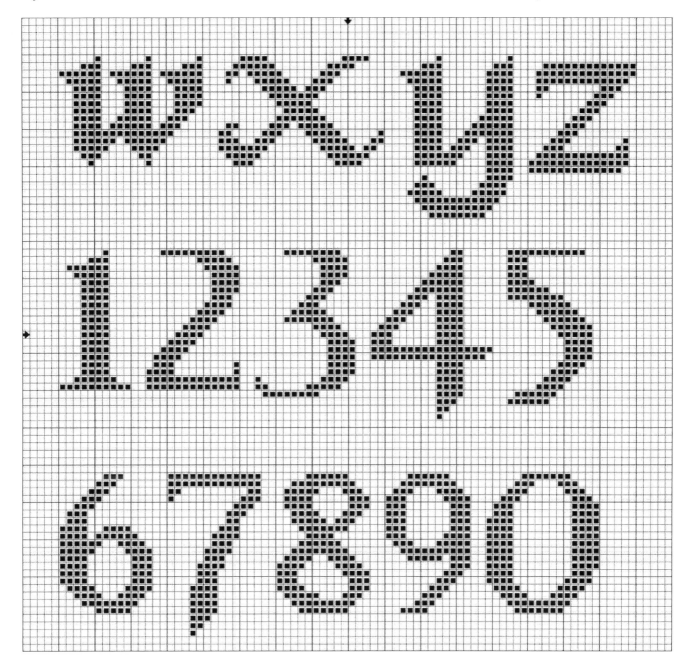

© 2000, 2019 Tink Boord-Dill   Permission is granted to enlarge single copy, solely for use as a Stitcher's Aid.

GRIDS
and
GRAPHS

20th ANNIVERSARY EDITION

TB-DN

ALPHABETS
For Discerning Makers

Grids and Graphs for Needlework and Crafts

HOW TO USE THE GRIDS AND GRAPHS

These *Grids and Graphs* allow you to create accurate charts for many needlework and craft projects. They can be used to create original designs or to modify existing designs.

There are 3 different types of Grids/Graphs depicted in here.

Square Graphs - These Graphs are designed to be *true size** and the heavy, dark lines fall at 1 inch increments.

> They are useful for Counted Thread techniques, such as *Needlepoint* and *Counted Cross Stitch*, which have ground fabrics with the same thread count vertically and horizontally.

> The Graphs are true size, so simply choose the Grid size which matches the ground fabric.

> Depending on your design needs, the squares can represent an individual stitch or each line can represent a thread of the ground fabric.

Beading Grids - These Grids depict the bead layouts for *Loom, Peyote, Two Drop, Brick,* and *Comanche Techniques*.

> Since beading projects can be quite small, these grids are not actual size but are proportionally accurate, allowing design work in an easily viewed size.

Ratio Grids - These Grids provide a wide range of useful options when working on a project where the horizontal units are a different size than the vertical units, such as **Knitting**, **Crochet, Weaving,** and **Smocking**.

> These Grids have heavy, dark lines every 5 lines, as a counting aid.

> The first number of the Ratio refers to the Horizontal Units and the second refers to the Vertical Units.

> Remember that you can always turn a Grid 90° to increase it usefulness. For example, if a project is 5 units horizontally and 4 units vertically, spinning the 4:5 grid 90° will result in that ratio.

Grids and Graphs for Needlework and Crafts

These Grids are proportionally accurate. Using the reduction and enlargement capabilities of copy equipment, the proper Ratio Grid can be sized to scale, as needed.

Tips for Success

When using the Graphs and Grids in this book, never write directly on the pages. Work on photocopies and keep the pages as clean as possible.

NOTE – Copy machines and printers may enlarge or reduce the image slightly, so when a true size copy is needed, measure it carefully and adjust it as needed.

For projects where the fabric will be created, such as **Knitting, Crochet, Weaving,** and **Smocking**, first create a 6" x 6" sample with the same techniques and materials that will be used in the design. Wash and steam the sample the same way the final project will be finished. Take careful measurements in each direction and find the Grid which is closest to those measurements.

The fewer stitches per inch a technique has, the more stitches the sample should have, to make it as accurate as possible.

Remember that a Ratio is the relationship between 2 numbers, reduced to the smallest increment. The initial relationship of Horizontal Units to Vertical Units may not seem to fit one of the Ratio Grids, but may be the same when reduced. For instance, a Knitting Gauge of 16 stitches to 20 rows is actually a 4:5 ratio. With experimentation, the Ratio Grids can be reduced or enlarged to a true working size.

If you need an area larger than what is depicted in a particular graph, tape multiple copies together to get the size needed.

Note: Permission is granted for the owner of this book to copy the Graphs and Grids for personal use.

SQUARE GRIDS - 12 BY 12 GRID

SQUARE GRIDS - 13 BY 13 GRID

SQUARE GRIDS – 14 BY 14 GRID

SQUARE GRIDS – 18 BY 18 GRID

BEADING GRIDS - TWO DROP STITCH BEAD GRID

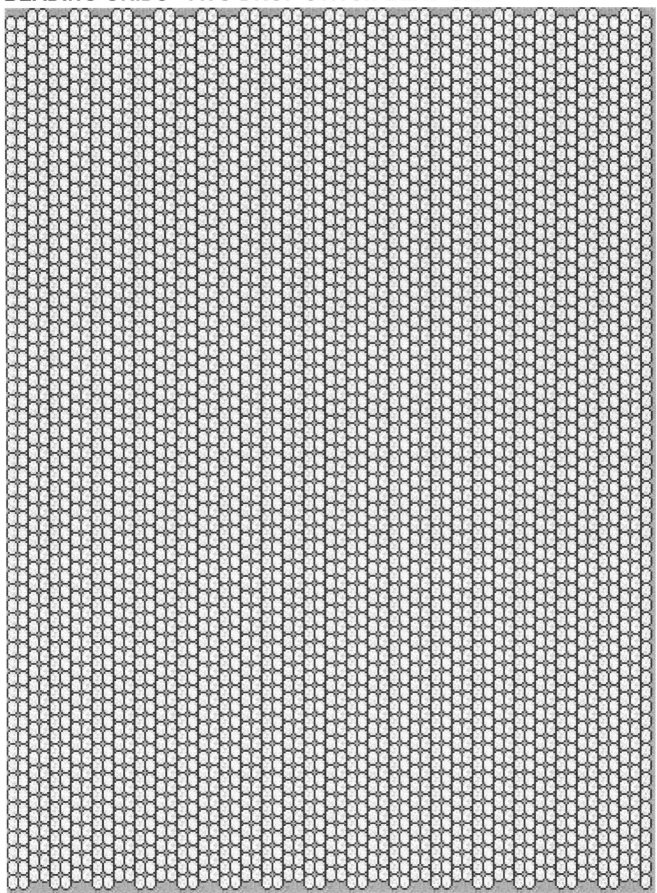

© 2019 Tink Boord-Dill, Tink Boord-Dill Needlework

TWO DROP BEAD GRID

BEADING GRIDS - BRICK STITCH BEAD GRID

© 2019, Tink Boord-Dill Needlework

BRICK BEAD GRID

BEADING GRIDS - COMANCHE STITCH BEAD GRID

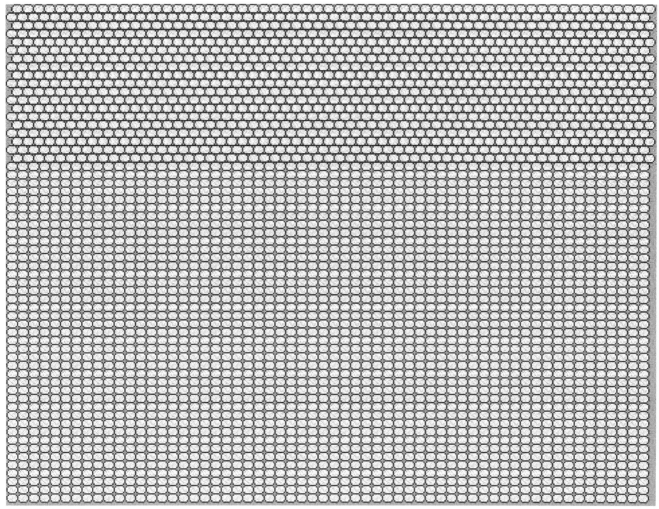

© 2019 Tink Boord-Dill Needlework

COMANCHE BEAD GRID

BEADING GRIDS - LOOM BEAD GRID

© 2019 Tink Boord-Dill Needlework

LOOM BEAD GRID

BEADING GRIDS - PEYOTE STITCH BEAD GRID

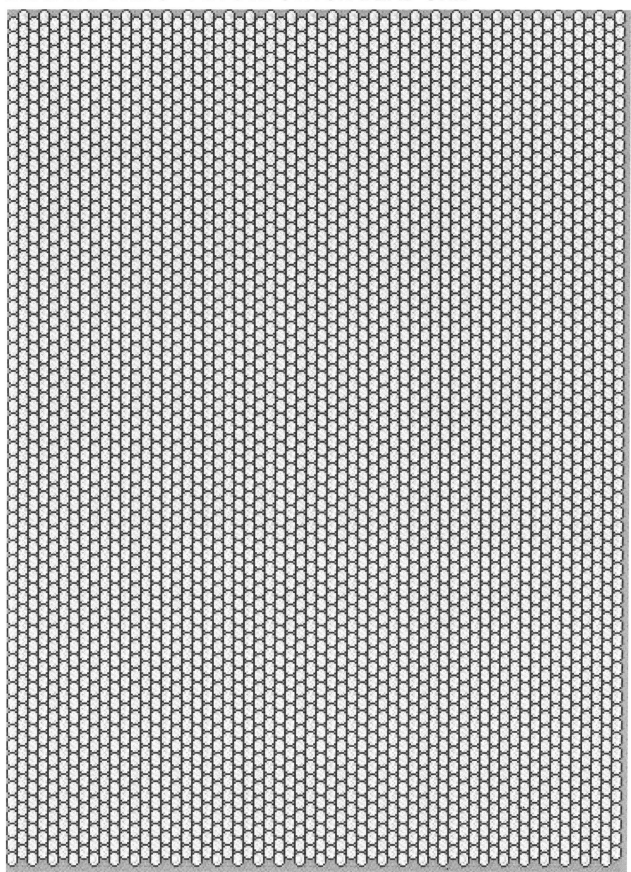

© 2019 Tink Boord-Dill Needlework

PEYOTE BEAD GRID

RATIO GRIDS - 2:3 GRID

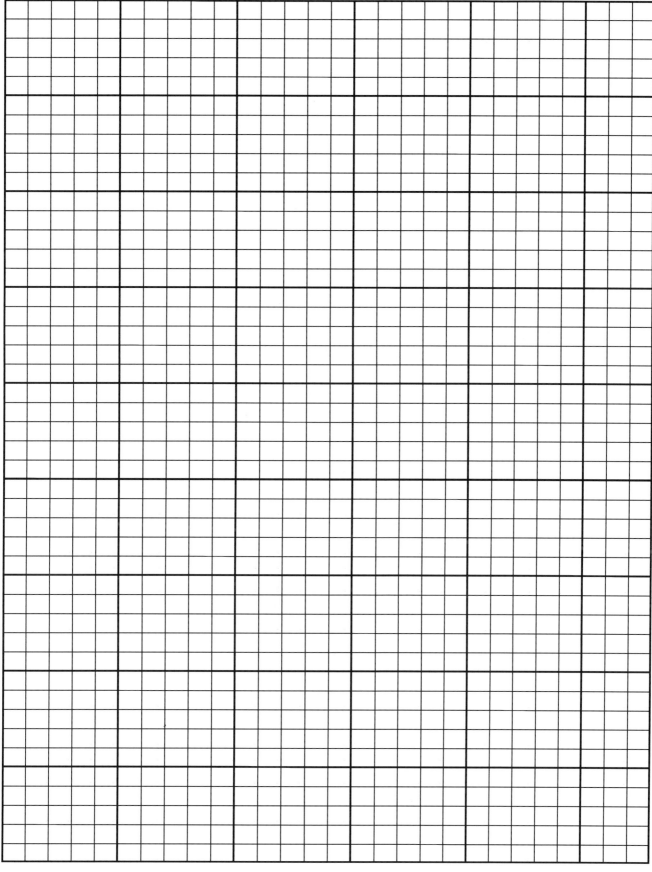

RATIO GRIDS - 4:5 GRID

Other Titles Available from
TINK BOORD-DILL NEEDLEWORK
Available as PRINT or DIGITAL

Get FREE Alphabets

NEWSLETTER Sign-up at www.TinkBD.com/a

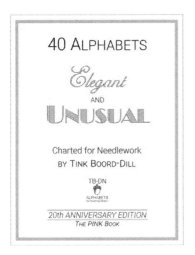

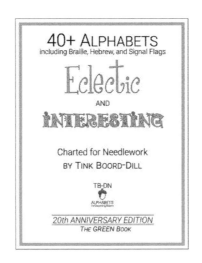

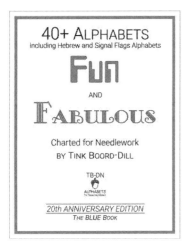

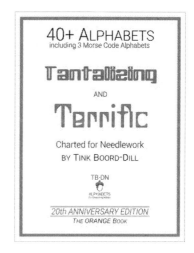

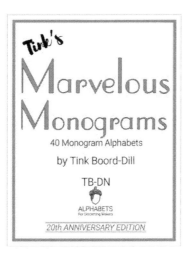

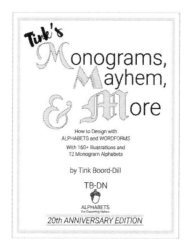

Made in the USA
San Bernardino, CA
31 October 2019

59196414R00109